Immaculate work in combed wheat reed at Roxton, Bedfordshire.

THATCH AND THATCHING

Jacqueline Fearn

Shire Publications Ltd

CONTENTS

Published in 1995 by Shire Publications Ltd, Cromwell House, Church Street, Princes Risborough, Buckinghamshire HP27 9AA, UK.

Copyright © 1976 by Jacqueline Fearn. First edition 1976; reprinted 1978, 1981, 1985, 1987, 1992 and 1995. Shire Album 16. ISBN 0 85263 337 8.

Printed in Great Britain by CIT Printing Services, Press Buildings, Merlins Bridge, Haverfordwest, Dyfed SA61 1XF.

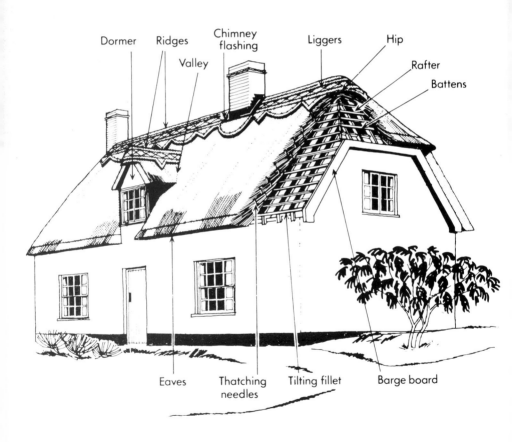

The principal features of a thatched roof.

Long straw cottages at Rowlands Castle, Hampshire.

INTRODUCTION

Most of us would agree that the presence of a thatched cottage in a view of the countryside adds a satisfying final touch. With its association with the unhurried past, it completes the rural scene as we think it should be. Occasionally there is the added pleasure of seeing a thatcher at work on a roof which is being splendidly renewed in bright straw or reed the colour of tarnished gold. Most people so rarely see a thatcher that it is not generally appreciated that thatching is a reasonably thriving craft: there is a course for apprentices at Knustone Hall in Northamptonshire and a National Federation of Master Thatchers Associations.

Any kind of roofing material was called *thaec* by the Saxons, and the act of applying it was *theccan*. As the commonest materials were vegetable - straw, reed, heather, bracken, turf - *thatch* came eventually to signify vegetable roofing. Until the seventeenth century, thatch was the most widespread form of roofing in Britain and it continued unchallenged in some areas until much later. It was not unknown for large and important buildings to be thatched, like Pevensey Castle in the fourteenth century and many churches, particularly in East Anglia. But thatch was most suitable for smaller buildings, not only because it was readily available and inexpensive but also because cheap walls and rafters could more easily support the light thatching material, and because extras like guttering and drain-pipes were unnecessary. The major drawback, however, was the risk of fire, particularly in towns. In London it was compulsory by 1212 to give thatch a coat of whitewash to protect it from sparks and new houses thereafter were not allowed to be thatched. Other towns followed suit in due course, sometimes prompted by a serious fire, as at Wareham in Dorset, where thatch was prohibited only after the fire of 1762. Thatching therefore became a country craft, as seems most appropriate to us.

A thatcher would usually have been a part-timer, employed on other jobs until his thatching skills were required. He did not only thatch buildings: until twenty or so years ago the thatcher was always in demand in arable areas to thatch the ricks. Sadly a thatched rick is an uncommon sight these days, except in the hill districts of Wales, where stacks of cut sheaves are stored in outlying places for the cattle, and in eastern Scotland where oats, raised on wooden frames or staddle stones, may be stored under thatch. Rick-thatching was a part of the great traditional thanksgiving for the harvest, a special and highly competitive job. Neighbouring farms vied to produce the smartest rickyard, and the thatcher's work, proudly ornamented with straw cocks, orbs and other insignia or corn dollies, supplied the crowning glory. Mechanisation and polythene have eliminated the thatcher from the farmyard.

In recent years, however, the number of full-time thatchers at work has stabilised at between five hundred and six hundred. This seems strange at first as a thatched roof is expensive and a small cottage can cost a great deal to re-roof. But people have become very conscious of the desirability of preserving the countryside and its crafts, and bodies like the Council for Small Industries in Rural Areas (COSIRA), formerly the Rural Industries Bureau, have given constructive assistance and local councils have encouraged and sometimes subsidised the rethatching of houses. In addition the ownership of many picturesque cottages has passed from the indigenous inhabitants, who could not afford the now expensive luxury of thatch, to the more affluent immigrants from towns who can. So the thatcher can often find plenty of local work and, through his regional association and COSIRA, work further afield should he need it. Young men are now being attracted by the independent outdoor life and the good financial prospects.

In many cases, though, one finds that thatching runs in the family, one of the few remaining crafts where skill is handed on in this way. Thatchers are usually individualists, independent of spirit and physically tough; working on a ladder in all weathers - only snow and heavy rain deter a thatcher - requires stamina and it is a solitary, uncomfortable position to maintain, standing with the body twisted, dealing with apparently intractable materials, and gauging with admirable skill by hand and eye alone. A thatcher often has an assistant working on the ground preparing the thatch but it is unusual to find two master thatchers on one roof, unless it is a very big job or unless they are, say, father and son. Methods of application are surprisingly uniform all over the country but the finished roofs vary considerably. This, of course, depends on the type of thatch and to some extent on regional tradition, but in areas where one or two thatching families have been at work for generations there is usually a distinctive style in thatching, noticeable mainly in the treatment of ridges, dormers and surface decoration. There is often no need to adorn the ridge with a trademark, such as a pheasant shaped in straw. Unity of style, however, is fast disappearing outside the South-west and Norfolk.

An immaculate range of thatched ricks from a bygone age.

THATCHING MATERIALS

For centuries, the most common material everywhere was the straw left after harvesting wheat, rye, oats or barley, and called long straw. Rye was the favourite but wheat straw the most generally used, oat and barley straw only being used as a last resort. Wheat for thatching is best harvested when slightly green so that it is not brittle and yields a little in handling, and a winter-grown crop is the best. The straw used generally to be ricked, sold by weight and sorted out on site when required. Unfortunately, good long straw has been progressively harder to come by as the combine harvester and

baler break up the straw, making it unsuitable for thatching. So the straw must still be cut with the old-fashioned binder. If the harvest could be brought in without breaking the stalks, modern high-yield wheat crops are too short in the stem and too pithy in the centre to please the thatcher. Some farmers set aside a few acres for growing the long-stemmed varieties which the thatchers may arrange to harvest themselves, endeavouring to keep down costs by returning the grain to the farmer after careful threshing.

It has been said that some cottages look more thatched than others, indicating a

noticeable difference and, perhaps, a more rustic finish. Long straw is distinctive: the straw is applied lengthwise, like hair on the head, giving a gentle, moulded pie-crust appearance, and the eaves and barges are always finished with long runners or liggers. The difficulty of obtaining straw is one reason why long-straw thatchers have had to consider the two other longer-lasting forms of thatching, Norfolk reed and Devon or combed wheat reed, and use different methods of application.

The finest material is Norfolk reed (*Phragmites communis*). It grows in water, the best in salt water, and is most common in marshy estuaries, principally in Norfolk. It grows from four to eight feet tall and can only be harvested after the frost has killed the long leaves or 'flag' on the main stem. In practice the reed is rarely cut before December and harvesting continues through the winter months until the young shoots begin to appear in March and April. Regular, if not annual, cutting is the only method of cultivation, as the straight, sturdy structure of the reed is impaired when it has stood in ever thickening bunches for a number of years. Wading through the icy water to cut reed with a scythe or sickle was an uninviting and slow job, and useful areas of reed remained uncut. Happily the Rural Industries Bureau (now COSIRA), working with local advice, devised a mechanical means of cutting which speeded up the process. After cutting, the reed is tied into bundles of twelve inches in diameter and stacked in 'fathoms' or groups of six.

Unlike long straw, Norfolk reed is laid so that only the sharp ends of the stalk are exposed. The ends bristle outwards so that water is shed from tip to tip on its way down the roof.

An innovation at the beginning of the nineteenth century, widely adopted in the South-west, enabled a superior roof to be laid in straw. An iron-toothed comb was devised which combed wheat straw to produce the clean, aligned stems known as combed wheat reed or Devon reed, which

ABOVE: *Feeding the wheat on to the top tier of the reed comber.*

BELOW LEFT: *Wheat reed leaving the comber and descending to the tyer at the bottom.*

BELOW RIGHT: *Bundling drawn-out long straw into yealms. Several yealms are already assembled in the yoke on the left.*

LEFT: *Splitting the hazel 'spar-gadd' with a spar hook.* RIGHT: *Twisting the length of hazel to make a spar staple.*

were then laid in the same way as Norfolk reed with only the ends of the straw exposed, producing a longer-lasting, neater roof. Today the wheat is cut by binder and then passed through a reed comber attached to the threshing drum. The comber strips the heads, which go through the thresher, and combs the wheat, which, butt-ends aligned, is conveyed on belts to a tier and tied into bundles, each weighing about 28 lb, which are butted to level the ends and then trimmed. Modern heavy-headed wheats are as unsuitable for combed wheat reed thatching as for long straw and old-fashioned varieties have been grown specially, but the variety Maris Huntsman produces long, strong stems, as well as a high grain yield, and seems to be a popular compromise crop for farmers with thatchers to supply, and particularly for those whose straw will be processed through the reed comber.

Other materials still in limited use for thatching are sedge and heather. Sedge is always used to ridge Norfolk-reed roofs, but in the Fen Country whole roofs of sedge can occasionally be seen. Like Norfolk reed, sedge is a marsh plant with a rougher, rush-like leaf. Ideally it is cut when green and easy to handle, although it can be cut all the year round. Heather was once in general use in non-corn-growing areas such as Dartmoor, the North-east

and Scotland. It was cut in autumn while still in bloom and laid with the roots intertwined and pointing upwards. Heather thatch can still be seen, particularly in parts of Scotland. Its least attractive feature, perhaps, is the heavy black colour the heather turns to as it dries.

Hazel wood is used for spar-making. Spars are of three types: long, one-inch-wide rods called sways which hold down the thatch; shorter half-inch-wide lengths which are twisted to make staples for packing the straw tightly together and securing at certain stages; and very long half-inch-wide lengths for the external liggers or runners which secure the ridge and, in long straw, the eaves and barges (gables).

The thatcher may cultivate his own hazel coppice and make all his own spars- an occupation for a rough day - but so many are needed that spar-making is a small industry in some areas. Although there is as yet no substitute for the small spars and external liggers, hazel sways are being replaced by some thatchers with lengths of mild tempered steel which will not be attacked by woodworm.

Temporary sways, to be removed as the work is permanently secured, are made from twisted straw or small handfuls of reed.

8

Rafters and battens ready for thatching. Note the tilting effect on the positioned reed of the projecting fascia board.

THE METHOD OF THATCHING

A roof which is to be thatched must include one or two special features. It must have a pitch of at least 50 degrees so that the rain will run off it easily, and the rafters must overhang the walls. Ideally a board called a tilting fillet should be fitted at right angles to the rafter at the eaves end in order to force the bottom layer of thatch out and up slightly. Battens are fixed horizontally across the rafters, at intervals at first of five inches and thereafter of nine inches until the last batten is about two inches from the vertical board at the ridge, which should stand up two inches above the converging rafters. At the gables a barge board nine

inches wide is fixed on the last rafter, which is fitted to overhang the gable by as much as ten inches. The barge board lies one and a half inches above the rafter level so that, like the tilting fillet, it forces the thatch up slightly. Windows have to be similarly treated and the areas round both the windows and the chimneys have to be prepared so that the thatch will flow evenly, enabling lead and cement seals to be inserted while the thatch retains an even pitch and the water flow is unimpeded.

If the roof has been thatched before, then the thatcher has two alternatives: either to strip the roof entirely before

9

rethatching, or, more usually, to strip an area which can be rethatched the same day, bearing in mind that battens may need repairing. As the straw underneath will be dry he rarely strips it all away and leaves a layer as a lining for the new work.

The thatcher needs to know before he starts work how much straw, wheat reed or Norfolk reed he will need, and the customer will almost certainly want an estimated cost. Generally the roof area is measured and the price assessed in terms of cost per 'square', which is 100 square feet. Regional thatching associations and COSIRA encourage such unit costing which is businesslike and reassuring for the customer. Not all thatchers like it, however, and some prefer to give an overall price.

BELOW: *A long-straw yoke.*
BOTTOM: *Hazel spars.*

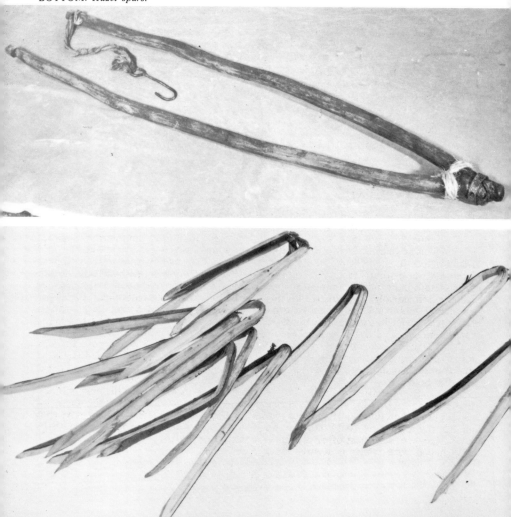

A side rake in use on long straw.

THE THATCHER'S TOOLS

Thatching tools vary according to the thatcher, the material in use and the locality, but the differences are marginal. It is possible to apply thatch without any special tools at all or with improvised ones; the craft lies in the skill of the thatcher. However, most thatchers will probably have certain basic items. They must have ladders and, ideally, the superb 48-rung wooden thatching ladders. These have the flat edges of their uprights outwards so that the thatcher does not rest his knee on a sharp edge, and the rungs are morticed into the rounds. Although big and difficult to transport, these ladders are still the best.

All thatch is sharp or prickly so the thatcher will often wear some protection, usually of leather, on his left, leaning arm, on his right, beating hand and on his knees. Long straw is most often carried in a V-shaped yoke which is secured by a leather thong or cord. Often some sort of cradle or 'horse', which can be fixed to the roof, is used to hold the material about to be used. Iron hooks and needles from six to twelve inches long are used to hold material in position and as levers to push the stalks close together. There are all sorts of knives and shearing hooks for cleaning down and trimming, but a long-straw thatcher will have a long-handled and long-bladed knife to trim the eaves. Reed thatch is dressed with a bat or leggatt. This consists of a handle attached to a rectangle of wood about ten inches by eight which is either ridged (for wheat reed) or nailed (for Norfolk reed) on the underside. A long-straw thatcher will also have a side rake to comb out the waste. All thatchers have shears and many have spot boards on which to bang the bunches to level the ends.

11

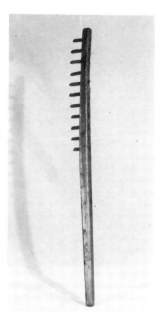

ABOVE LEFT: *A handful of thatching needles.*

ABOVE RIGHT: *A small rake for long straw.*

CENTRE: *Thatching shears.*

BOTTOM: *A special leggatt for use in difficult angles on combed wheat reed.*

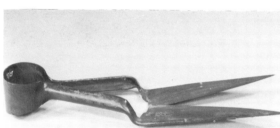

A ridge of Norfolk reed and sedge over slate.

THATCHING IN NORFOLK REED

The bunches of reed as delivered to the site will probably still need to be graded into long, short and coarse categories, long reed being needed for the eaves, short for the barges, and coarse for general work. Bundles twelve inches in diameter are assembled, banged or 'butted' on the spot board to level the ends, and tied. Four to eight bundles will be taken to the roof at a time.

Work begins at the eaves and proceeds from right to left. A staple is fixed in the corner to secure the binding twine for the first course, and the first bundles are butted to set a bevel for the overhang. Starting at an angle of 45 degrees with an overhang of two or three feet, bundles are fixed, large ends down, the cord passing once round the bundle and twice round the batten before being double tied. Each one is butted upwards with the leggatt to tighten the reed in the bond and forced tightly up to the next with the needles. At a gable the barge bunches are secured under a sway parallel to the barge and close to it to hold the reed under tension. There is an overhang of six inches. Handfuls of reed are forced under the small ends lying against the rafters to provide both a lever to hold the reed under tension and a tidy back-filling. The next course is laid well down over the first and swayed low down, temporarily with a reed bond and finally with a hazel or steel sway and iron hooks. The thatcher locates the rafter into which the hook is driven by probing with a

13

LEFT: *Butting Norfolk reed to put a bevel on the reed for the eaves course.*

RIGHT: *An eaves course in Norfolk reed; the 45-degree angle at the corner has straightened to vertical.*

needle. Succeeding courses are laid similarly, each completely covering the sway securing the lower course, the reed being continually dressed with the leggatt to keep the butt-ends in smooth alignment all the way up the roof.

Chimneys and windows need careful treatment to maintain the smooth lines and rain-shedding angles of the laid reed. The lead flashings above a free-standing chimney lead up under the thatch, which is cut off several inches from the chimney, forming a gully into which the water flows. The flashing extends over the thatch at the sides so the water runs on to the thatch. Alternatively the lead or cement is laid over the thatch and up round the chimney like a collar. Valleys, where two roofs meet, are packed with reed to form a smooth curve.

As the courses approach the ridge board, the tops of the reed project above it. Norfolk reed will not bend over the top of the ridge, so the ends are cut off at the same angle as the approaching rafters, level with the ridge, which is then prepared for the sedge ridging. The gables are trimmed and dressed with the leggatt, then a long roll of reed, the length of the ridge and from four inches in diameter, is assembled on the ground and then fixed to the ridge. At the apex of the barge, reed is laid horizontally and swayed down over the ridge. A thick layer of damp or green sedge is assembled over the ridge, in line with the ridge courses, to form a skirt, pushed tightly together and fastened down with spars driven into the reed. A narrower roll is sparred on top of the skirt into the first roll, and over this even yealms of sedge are bent to form a 'turnover' top. This is sparred firmly down with liggers about twelve inches apart and a vertical barge ligger. Any decorative diagonal liggers are sparred down and the edges of the skirt are trimmed into decorative shapes. The final tidying operation follows, with the clipping of odd ends and the removal of loose bits.

14

ABOVE LEFT: *The solid, neat gable of Norfolk reed taking shape—part of a full course, held down by a temporary sway.* ABOVE RIGHT: *Norfolk reed laid horizontally at the apex to provide a firm base for the sedge ridge.* BELOW LEFT: *Laying the final ridge course on a Norfolk reed roof, with sedge yealms drawn out over the top.* BELOW RIGHT: *Sparring down the beginning of the top ligger on a sedge ridge. The sedge will be pushed tightly under this ligger.*

RIGHT: *A gable in Norfolk reed with a pattern cut into the body of the roof as well as the ridge. Note the parallel lines of the reeds over the barge boards.*

BELOW LEFT: *Lead flashing fitted like a collar round the chimney and over the ridge.*

ABOVE: *A lead gutter behind a chimney, fitted under the thatch which will shed water into it for dispersal over the thatch below.*

Combed wheat reed cottages at Selworthy, Somerset.

THATCHING IN COMBED WHEAT REED

Combed wheat reed usually comes to the thatcher in the bundles or 'nitches' he will use. Each nitch should be tidied, butted on the spot board to even the ends, sprinkled with water through the top end and left to soak for a while.

The eaves and barges are laid with 'wadds', extra large handfuls of reed butted and then tied firmly together. The staple and cord are fixed in the corner and a hazel sway is nailed close to the barge board to provide a fixing for the barge wadds. The corner, angled wadd is tied in by lacing round the wadd, over the sway and then the batten, and pulling tight. The succeeding wadds are laced to the batten, the barge wadds to the sway. To align and tighten the wadds in the cord the butts are dressed with the leggatt as the work proceeds.

The courses are laid on a back-filling scattered over the battens. Half a nitch of reed is butted on the roof, laid in the corner and held in position with one arm while the butts are dressed into position. The reed is lightly swayed down and the butts are dressed with the leggatt. When sufficient reed is in place it is properly swayed down with a sway secured by an iron hook or by stitching. Each bunch is tightly packed next to another and held in place temporarily by an iron needle. The temporary sway is released as required.

The ridge is based on a tightly packed roll of reed about four inches thick and varying in length according to the ridge length. The tops of the course which oversail the ridge are twisted and folded back, the twisted knuckles being forced against each other and secured by a reed sway sparred into the ridge roll. At the apex wadds are laid thickly over the top and sparred into the roll. A second, smaller roll is sparred through into the first. The next, pattern course is laid with large handfuls of reed, their small ends

17

ABOVE: *Tying in the eaves bunches of combed wheat reed; note the barge sway, to which the barge bunches will be tied, and the hooks to push the work together.*

TOP RIGHT: *Dressing the eaves bunches of combed wheat reed to tighten them in the cord.*

CENTRE RIGHT: *Fixing the permanent sway. The rafter has been located with the needle and the hook is being positioned. Note the temporary straw sway below.*

BOTTOM RIGHT: *The yoke reed holder in use on the roof.*

ABOVE LEFT: *Butting the nitch on the roof to align and bevel the butts of wheat reed.*

ABOVE RIGHT: *Butting the ends of combed wheat reed with the leggatt.*

BELOW: *Sparring down combed wheat reed with a straw bond.*

folded under and placed so that they end just above the top of the roll, just meeting those laid on the other side of the roof. A third, small roll is now sparred down and a ligger is started to run across the ridge. The ridge course is laid by taking an evened-out bunch of reed, bending it in half and positioning it under the ligger. A vertical needle levers the reeds together. Side liggers are sparred into position six, six, then twelve inches apart. Cross liggers are decoratively positioned and the required pattern is cut at the ends. On a good ridge the top will be very narrow and the depth of thatch some eighteen inches. Finally there will be a last beating up with the leggatt and a light trim with the shearing hook.

Chimneys and dormers are treated in the same way as with Norfolk reed.

19

TOP RIGHT: *Twisting the oversailing ends of combed wheat reed at the ridge.*

CENTRE RIGHT: *The final side ligger on a combed wheat reed ridge being sparred down.*

BOTTOM RIGHT: *Trimming combed wheat reed with a shearing hook. Note the characteristic leaning position.*

BELOW: *Close-up view of the bristling finish of wheat reed.*

LEFT: *Cross-section through combed wheat reed, showing the construction of the courses and the ridge rolls. Norfolk reed and long straw would present a similar appearance, with differences as indicated in the text.*

RIGHT: *Cross-section showing the depth and construction of a wheat reed ridge.*

TOP LEFT: *Driving a spar horizontally through one long-straw bottle into the next to pack the straw tightly.*

CENTRE RIGHT: *Courses shown in steps across the roof, showing the well-covered positions of the sways.*

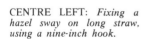

CENTRE LEFT: *Fixing a hazel sway on long straw, using a nine-inch hook.*

BOTTOM RIGHT: *Side-raking a section of work in long straw. Note the new battens.*

A highly decorated long-straw ridge near Eye, Suffolk, with an unusual rolled barge.

THATCHING IN LONG STRAW

Of the various types of thatching material, long straw needs most preparation before it can be laid. It is usually spread out in layers which are thoroughly wetted and then left to soak for an hour or two to make the straw pliable. Then, working in a straight line, handfuls of straw are drawn out evenly, tidied so that the straws are in line and gathered into bunches which are thicker at the bottom than at the top. These are 'yealms' and are about eighteen inches wide and five inches deep. As they are assembled they are laid, large end forward, in a Y-shaped yoke which holds up to eight yealms. Special, wide yealms called 'bottles' are made for the eaves; these have a splayed large end and are folded double and tied at the bent end.

Work begins at the eaves and the roof is completed in sections, some thatchers staggering the courses across the roof, others working upwards in lanes about thirty inches wide. The first bottles are laid at 45 degrees and overhang by half the three-foot length. The bottle may be tied in with tarred cord or swayed down by a sway held by hooks driven into the rafter

as low as possible or sometimes into the wall plate. Each bottle is driven hard towards the previous one by spars driven horizontally through the straw. The barge is treated similarly, the barge sway and first bottle being wedged under the eaves sway for a tight join. On this bristling fringe the roof courses are built up.

A thin layer of straw is laid over the battens as a tidy lining, and then the first roof course is started at the same angle as and very low on the bottle and is sparred down just below the eaves sway with a twisted straw bond. This makes a double course to give the desired eaves thickness of up to eighteen inches. Succeeding courses are laid overlapping the previous one by two thirds and are permanently swayed down after every two courses. The straw is tightly pushed between needles, and each section is tidied and often side-raked.

When the ridge is reached, a roll of straw is tied on to the ridge board and more bottles are swayed down around the apex. The last yealms are sparred into each side, the small ends which meet above the ridge being sparred into the roll. For the ridge course, yealms are drawn out and equalised at top and bottom, bent across the apex and forced tightly down. The top ligger is laid along the ridge and sparred down. Three liggers are secured on either side. The barge liggers meet and form a point underneath which it may be necessary to pack more straw before finally fixing. The barges are then cut with the long-handled knife and trimmed with shears. Finally, the main body of the roof and the eaves are raked and neatly trimmed.

Wire netting is always necessary to protect a long-straw roof from birds; it may then last up to twenty years, though it will probably need to be re-ridged every ten years and patched in places.

TOP LEFT: *Fixing the barge ligger; where two lengths join, their ends are held together under a spar.*

BOTTOM LEFT: *Laying a good foundation for the ridge course. Note the ridge roll in position.*

ABOVE LEFT: *Pushing the straw of the bent yealms together with a needle to make a tight ridge.*

ABOVE RIGHT: *Trimming a long-straw gable with a long-handled knife, allowing an overhang of about four inches.*

BELOW: *An unusually shaggy long-straw roof — all trimming has been left to the end.*

Rethatching in heather.

Reconstruction of a Saxon hut at the Weald and Downland Open Air Museum, Singleton, West Sussex.

CHOOSING AND LIVING WITH THATCH

It is said that one must go to Norfolk to see thatching at its best and from the practical and technical point of view, in the satisfaction derived from immaculate roofs of long-lasting material, this is true. Norfolk reed is ideal for its purpose, being long, tough and straight, allowing no gaps in the imperceptibly mingled blocks of reed. It is laid, perfectly positioned and skilfully shaped around windows and valleys, to produce a tailored, dependable-looking finish, enormously enhancing a building. It will often last a lifetime. Combed wheat reed, though not so long-lasting, so much resembles Norfolk reed as to be indistinguishable at first glance, particularly in recently thatched roofs.

The difference is detectable in the sedge ridge of Norfolk-reed roofs and in the cutting to shape around windows and at the eaves of combed wheat reed. In parts of Devon and Somerset local styles of tapered eaves and dormers give the roofs a distinctive daintiness of appearance which is very pleasing. West Country gable and porch pinnacles, too, have a gay, light and nautical air.

But not all houses benefit from the precise lines imposed by the reeds, particularly Norfolk reed. Small cottages can appear too smart and box-like, small dormers disproportionately bulky, differing roof-heights too pronounced. This is where long straw is pre-eminent

ABOVE: *A housing estate at Winterton-on-Sea, Norfolk, thatched in Norfolk reed.*

BELOW: *Dorset reed or 'Abbotsbury spear' bound lengthwise over roofs in Abbotsbury, Dorset – a repair, but long-lasting nevertheless.*

A wooden shed trimly thatched in heather.

and will be missed if it disappears, imparting as it can a gentle elegance and fluid line. Certainly this is the romantic, Gothic roof so dear to the nineteenth-century landscape designer and artist, so necessary to the planned view.

As most home-owners require a practical, trouble-free roof, not merely an eyecatcher, they will consider, if they can afford to, which material is the best investment. Unfortunately long straw, though the cheapest to lay, will need to be replaced much sooner than Norfolk reed and appreciably sooner than combed wheat reed. Estimates of lifespan vary, but where all three are well laid, properly maintained and not subjected to extreme wet, long straw will last from ten to twenty years, combed wheat reed from twenty to forty years and Norfolk reed between fifty and seventy years. Of course some houses boast thatch which has lasted longer than average - Norfolk reed has lasted a cen-

tury, as has some of the curiously laid Abbotsbury 'spear' or reed of Dorset (this reed appears to be laid like long straw but it has still lasted). In its lifetime each roof will need to be re-ridged at least once and may need patching.

One thatcher said he would thatch round a wheelbarrow if he found it on the roof at the appropriate pitch with battens in place; he regarded thatch as an appropriate roof for any type of building. However, it is uncommon to see a thatched roof on brick walls - if you try to visualise it you will see why that is a good thing - and it has predominated in the areas of cob-mud and clay-lump wall construction, such as Devon (it is a light roof for frail walls), and looks particularly well with limewashed and pastel walls as in East Anglia. Timber-clad and half-timbered walls set it off and it is not out of place with stone, as the moorland areas show. Where it did decline most sharply in

RIGHT: *Wheat reed replacing long straw near Tring in Hertfordshire.*

LEFT: *The windmill at High Ham in Somerset, with a thatched cap.*

A thatched stack of old sheep hurdles on the village green at Priddy in Somerset. The village has held an annual sheep fair for over six hundred years and local legend claims that the fair will cease if these old hurdles are removed.

popularity, such as in the industrial North and West, the availability of slate and clay tiles complemented the desire for roofing which would withstand wetter weather conditions than those of the South and East better than traditional long straw.

Nowadays most roofs, except those of Norfolk reed, will be covered at some stage in their lives with wire or nylon netting to keep out the birds. This it does very well but it can form a trap for falling leaves which encourage damp, and these ought to be removed. After all, the thatcher has carefully shaped the thatch over or under chimney flashing and packed the valleys to form gentle shedding lines, his whole craft devoted to the efficient shedding of water by a material which might be expected to absorb it. In a proper state of repair, thatch will never be wet beyond an inch or two of its thickness and the original colour of fresh straw or reed is revealed underneath when the roof is stripped for rethatching.

Fire is a hazard to any property but obviously thatch will burn very much more readily than most other forms of roof. Insurance companies are very conscious of this and charge up to five times as much for thatched houses and their contents. However, with modern fuel it is unusual for sparks and embers to fly out of the chimney and so set fire to the roof. So the inhabitants must exercise the same care to prevent internal fires as anyone else - it is worse with thatch, but any fire is bad. There is a fire-retardant solution in which reed or straw can be soaked before use but it does not appear to have been used very often.

The final word on thatch must be said from the inside. There is no pleasanter roof to live under - it provides excellent insulation to keep the warmth in during the winter and out during the summer. Often it is associated with sloping ceilings in the bedrooms which, with their thatch covering and protected windows, are quiet because thatch also soundproofs very well. This apparently archaic form of roof still provides the most comfortable protection from the weather.

PLACES TO VISIT

The museums below have good collections of tools and exhibits relating to rural crafts, including thatching.

Avoncroft Museum of Buildings, Stoke Heath, Bromsgrove, Worcestershire B60 4JR. Telephone: 01527 831363/831886.

Bewdley Museum, The Shambles, Load Street, Bewdley, Worcestershire DY12 2AE. Telephone: 01299 403573.

Breamore Countryside Museum, Breamore, Fordingbridge, Hampshire SP6 2DF. Telephone: 01725 512468.

Chiltern Open Air Museum, Newland Park, Gorelands Lane, Chalfont St Giles, Buckinghamshire HP8 4AD. Telephone: 01494 871117; information 0494 872163.

Dorset County Museum, High West Street, Dorchester, Dorset DT1 1XA. Telephone: 01305 262735.

Museum of East Anglian Life, Abbots Hall, Stowmarket, Suffolk IP14 1DL. Telephone: 01449 612229.

Museum of English Rural Life, The University, Whiteknights, Reading, Berkshire RG6 2AG. Telephone: 01734 318660.

Museum of Lakeland Life and Industry, Abbot Hall, Kendal, Cumbria LA9 5AL. Telephone: 01539 722464.

Museum of Lincolnshire Life, The Old Barracks, Burton Road, Lincoln LN1 3LY. Telephone: 01522 528448.

Museum of Wiltshire Rural Life, The Great Barn, Avebury, Wiltshire SN8 1RF. Telephone: 01672 539555.

Norfolk Rural Life Museum and Union Farm, Beech House, Gressenhall, Dereham, Norfolk NR20 4DR. Telephone: 01362 860563.

North Cornwall Museum and Gallery, The Cleave, Camelford, Cornwall. Telephone: 01840 212954.

Oxfordshire County Museum, Fletcher's House, Park Street, Woodstock, Oxfordshire OX7 1SN. Telephone: 01993 811456.

Rutland County Museum, Catmos Street, Oakham, Rutland, Leicestershire LE15 6HW. Telephone: 01572 723654.

Ulster American Folk Park, Melton Road, Castletown, Omagh, County Tyrone, Northern Ireland BT78 5QY. Telephone: 01662 243292.

Weald and Downland Open Air Museum, Singleton, Chichester, West Sussex PO18 0EU. Telephone: 01243 811348.

FURTHER READING

Brockett, Peter, and Wright, Adela. *The Care and Repair of Thatched Roofs*. Technical Pamphlet 10, Society for the Protection of Ancient Buildings, 37 Spital Square, London E1 6DY.

Thatch. Magazine of the Thatch Advisory Service, 29 Nine Mile Ride, Finchampstead, Wokingham, Berkshire RG11 4QD.

Thatch: A Manual for Owners, Surveyors, Architects and Builders. David and Charles, 1987.

The Thatcher's Craft, Rural Development Commission, reprinted 1988.

ACKNOWLEDGEMENTS
The author wishes to thank for their help and guidance Andrew Jewell, then Keeper, and Dr Sadie B. Ward of the Museum of English Rural Life at Reading, members of the staff at the Council for Small Industries in Rural Areas, and Mr C. Purser, Master Thatcher, of Woburn, Bedfordshire. The drawing on page 2 is by Ron Shaddock. Photographs are acknowledged as follows: Council for Small Industries in Rural Areas, pages 3, 6, 9, 12 (top left and bottom), 14 (both), 15 (all), 16 (all), 18 (all), 20 (top and centre), 21 (both), 22 (top, centre left and centre right), 23, 24 (both), 25 (top left and top right), 29; Cadbury Lamb, pages 17, 27, 28 (both) and 30 (both); London News Agency, page 25 (bottom); Mid Essex Reporting Agency, Witham, page 22 (bottom); Museum of English Rural Life, Reading, pages 1, 5, 7 (all), 8 (both), 10 (both), 11, 12 (top right and centre), 13, 19 (all), 20 (left and bottom right), 26; Mrs E. Preston, page 31. The cover illustration is from 'The Thatcher' by G. Morland.